CHEFS

BY EMMA LESS

AMICUS READERS ● AMICUS INK

amicus
readers

Amicus Readers and Amicus Ink are imprints of Amicus
P.O. Box 1329, Mankato, MN 56002
www.amicuspublishing.us

Cataloging-in-Publication Data is on file with the Library of Congress.
ISBN 978-1-68151-290-7 (library binding)
ISBN 978-1-68152-272-2 (paperback)
ISBN 978-1-68151-352-2 (eBook)

Editor: Valerie Bodden
Designer: Patty Kelley

Photo Credits:
Cover: Andresr/iStock
Interior: Dreamstime.com: Glenda Powers 3, Bowie15 4, Tyler Olson 6, Erwin Purnomo Sidi 9. Shutterstock: Dan Kosmayer 10, Lesterair 12, Lilke 15, Bolygomaki 16T, Piotr Pawinski 16R, Terrace Studio 16B.

Printed in China.

HC 10 9 8 7 6 5 4 3 2 1
PB 10 9 8 7 6 5 4 3 2 1

Jan wants to be a chef.
What does a chef do?

A chef wears a hat and an apron. They keep her clothes clean.

The chef plans
what to cook.
He chooses
good food.

The food is kept
in a big, cold room.
The cold keeps
food fresh.

Today, the chef makes soup. She tastes it. Yum!

Look at this cake!
It has
frosting flowers!

What are you

cooking, Mary?
Looks like

a pizza!

pot

stove

knife